Where Is
the Empire State Building?

by Janet B. Pascal

illustrated by Daniel Colón

Grosset & Dunlap
An Imprint of Penguin Group (USA) LLC

To my mama. Like the Empire State Building,
she will always be the best beloved—JBP

GROSSET & DUNLAP
Published by the Penguin Group
Penguin Group (USA) LLC, 375 Hudson Street, New York, New York 10014, USA

USA | Canada | UK | Ireland | Australia | New Zealand | India | South Africa | China

penguin.com
A Penguin Random House Company

The publisher does not have any control over and does not assume any responsibility for
author or third-party websites or their content.

Library of Congress Cataloging-in-Publication Data is available.

ISBN 978-0-448-48426-6   10 9 8 7 6 5 4 3

Contents

Where Is the Empire State Building?

In 1929, there was a "race for the sky" in New York City. Two new skyscrapers were going up—the Chrysler Building and the Manhattan Company Building. Each owner wanted his building to be the tallest in the world. But neither man knew exactly what height the other was aiming for. The owner of the Manhattan Company managed to discover the plans for the Chrysler Building. Immediately, he changed his plans so that his building would be taller.

So in April 1930, the Manhattan Company Building became the tallest in the world. But only for a few weeks. Secretly, the crew of the Chrysler Building was creating a tall spire. All the work took place inside the unfinished building, so no one knew about it. When the spire—125 feet high—was finished, it was lifted up through a hole in the roof. Suddenly the tallest building in the world was the Chrysler Building! With its spire, it was 1,046 feet tall.

What neither company knew that a third group of builders was watching them both closely. Their building was already designed. But they were waiting until the Chrysler Building was finished before making their plans final. However tall the Chrysler Building was, they planned to make sure their own building was a little taller.

This new skyscraper was the Empire State Building. It stands in the heart of New York City, with its front entrance on Fifth Avenue below Thirty-Fourth Street. It is 102 stories high and 1,250 feet tall—1,454 feet if you count the antenna on top, which was added later. Decorated with aluminum and stainless steel, it soars above other nearby skyscrapers, gleaming in the sun.

For forty years—longer than any other

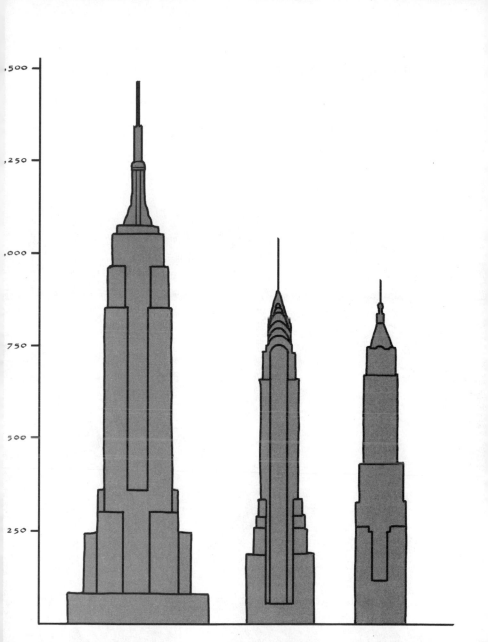

,500		
,250		
,000		
750		
500		
250		

Empire State
Building

Chrysler
Building

Manhattan
Company Building

building—it held the title of the world's tallest building. Today, most people no longer even know what the world's tallest building is. But everyone still knows the Empire State Building.

It is one of the world's best-loved buildings. An average of ten thousand people from all over the world visit it every day. People everywhere recognize it from movies, pictures, and advertisements. For most people, it symbolizes New York City.

CHAPTER 1
From Farm to Skyscraper

Only one hundred years before work on the Empire State Building started, the spot where it would stand was still countryside. In Manhattan in 1827, William Astor bought a little farm there, with a peaceful stream running through it.

Astor was one of the richest businessmen in America. One way he made money was by buying cheap land that he guessed would soon be worth a lot. He was sure New York City would quickly grow to surround his farm— and he was right.

By the 1850s, the area had become a fashionable neighborhood. William Astor's two sons built themselves mansions on the lot, and the Astor family moved up to Thirty-Fourth Street. Their move turned the area into a center of power and wealth. It has stayed so ever since.

The Four Hundred

As the wife of one of America's richest and most powerful men, Mrs. Caroline Astor ruled New York's fashionable society from her mansion. She decided who deserved to be a member of high society and who did not. So, everyone wanted her approval. Only the "best people" could pass her exclusive doors.

The largest room in Caroline Astor's mansion held about four hundred people. This meant when she gave a ball, only four hundred people could be invited. If you were invited, it showed you were important. If not, you were second-class. For this reason, fashionable society in New York was often referred to as "the Four Hundred."

By the 1890s, the branches of the Astor family living in the two mansions were fighting. Each Mrs. Astor thought that she should be the most important lady in the family. They both wanted to be known as *the* Mrs. Astor. The newspapers loved reporting on this battle.

Things got so bad that William Waldorf Astor and his wife moved away. He built a hotel where his house had stood. He did this to spite Caroline Astor, his aunt, who lived in the other house. The tall hotel blocked her sunlight. And he knew she would hate travelers coming and going right next to her.

Caroline did indeed hate the Waldorf Hotel. Soon after it opened, she moved. Her son turned the site of her mansion into another hotel: the Astoria. Before long, the two warring hotels were joined together to create one huge, fancy place—the Waldorf-Astoria Hotel. When it opened, it was the world's largest hotel. In "Peacock Alley,"

Waldorf Hotel

the long hall that joined the two buildings, upper-class New Yorkers and visitors strolled along in elegant clothes and jewels, showing off.

The city continued growing, however. Soon, businesses began moving into the area. Poor people came to work in small factories. Machines created smoke and dirt. The area was no longer so upper-class.

By 1928, it was time for the Waldorf-Astoria to move to a better neighborhood. The land where it stood was worth a lot of money. It took up almost a whole city block. By now, it was nearly impossible to buy a lot that big in the middle of New York City.

The Waldorf-Astoria was sold for about $16 million. This was the biggest real-estate sale of the year. By then, everyone was constructing tall buildings. Where William Astor's farm once stood, there would be a skyscraper.

The New Waldorf-Astoria

The Waldorf-Astoria was a beloved part of high-society life. When it was sold, people mourned its loss. The owners wanted to continue the traditions of the original hotel in a better location. In 1931, they opened the new Waldorf-Astoria on Park Avenue. With forty-seven stories, it was the tallest hotel in the world. It had its own entrance to Grand Central Terminal so important guests could board their trains without having to mix with the crowds. The architects made sure to include a new version of the famous Peacock Alley. In 1949, the hotel began spelling its name with a double hyphen—Waldorf=Astoria—to symbolize Peacock Alley.

CHAPTER 2
How to Build a Tall Building

Throughout history, whenever a better method of construction was invented, buildings became taller. The earliest builders used the post and lintel system. Two posts stand upright. A stone called a *lintel* is balanced across the top of them. Stonehenge in England is one good example. The posts had to stand fairly close together because a lintel couldn't be made too long. It would just crack down the middle. This limited the size of buildings.

The ancient Romans were able to build much higher by using arches. An arch could hold up a lot of weight. In fact, the more weight was piled on it, the stronger it became.

The cathedral builders of the Middle Ages invented several new forms of arches. They used them to create huge cathedrals that soared skyward. However, arches only worked for big, open spaces. Huge buildings had to be mostly empty inside. It wasn't possible to make tall buildings with lots of different floors. If floors ran all the way across the space, they would collapse.

In modern cities, buildings with many stories were needed. But until the 1880s, buildings could be ten stories high, at the most. All the weight of a building was held up by the bottom of the outside walls. So the taller a building got, the thicker the walls had to be. Eventually the walls would have to be so thick that there would be no floor space left.

In the 1850s, people started to build walls on an open framework of cast iron. Iron was stronger than wood or stone. In a cast-iron building, the walls look like a cage of iron columns and arches. This framework holds up all the weight of the building. The wall covering the frame is called a *curtain wall*, because it hangs from the frame like a curtain. All it has to do is block out wind and water. It doesn't have to carry any weight. That means it can be made very thin and light. The curtain wall is like the skin on a body. The iron framework is the skeleton that holds everything in shape.

It was easier and cheaper to build tall cast-iron buildings than tall stone buildings. The height of the building didn't affect the thickness of the walls. However, even using cast iron, it still wasn't possible to build skyscrapers. The tallest cast-iron buildings were only ten or eleven stories high, not much taller than stone buildings. Iron was brittle. When it got much taller than ten stories, the iron framework might crack. If builders used steel instead of iron, they could make the framework as tall as they wanted. Steel is iron combined with carbon and other elements. It is much stronger than iron. It is also more flexible, so it doesn't break as easily.

Unfortunately, making steel was much too slow and expensive. No one knew a good way to make pieces large enough for a tall building. That changed in 1855. An English inventor named Henry Bessemer figured out a quick and easy way to make large steel beams. Bessemer's beams didn't cost much more than iron beams.

Henry
Bessemer

Home Insurance Building, Chicago

Suddenly there was almost no limit on how tall a building could be. A new name was invented for tall buildings: *skyscrapers*. New Yorkers hate to admit it, but the first real skyscraper was not built in New York City. It was the Home Insurance Building in Chicago, finished in 1885.

Skyscrapers

There is no exact height at which a building becomes a skyscraper. Originally the word was used for anything that rose so high it seemed to touch the sky. Big hats, ships with tall sails, or even very tall men might be called skyscrapers. In the 1870s and 1880s, people were so amazed by the new buildings going up in Chicago and New York that they started using the word to mean a tall building.

In New York, people were slow to welcome skyscrapers. They seemed too tall—and too dangerous. What if they blew over in a high wind? One of the city's earliest steel frame skyscrapers was the Tower Building. (It was torn down in 1913.) Begun in 1888, it was eleven stories high. To convince people it was safe, the architect climbed all the way to the top of the framework during a storm. Then he dropped a line with a weight on it down the middle. The line didn't swing back and forth at all. This proved that the building would stand up to the winds outside.

People soon came to trust the new steel skeletons. In 1883 the famous Brooklyn Bridge opened in New York City. Everyone felt safe crossing it because it was held up by huge, solid stone towers. By 1901, building had started on the Manhattan Bridge a little farther north. This bridge had steel towers, not stone ones. The builders originally thought they might cover the steel framework with granite, to make the towers look like they were built of stone. But they didn't have to. By now people believed in the strength of steel towers.

CHAPTER 3
Up and Up

Using steel, it was possible to construct a building twenty-five stories high. But who would want to use such a building? No one would want to walk up all those stairs every day. First, builders needed a practical elevator.

Elevators had been around for a while, but people didn't think they were safe enough to carry people in tall buildings. What if the cable holding the elevator broke? The people inside would fall hundreds of feet to their death.

Then in 1852, Elisha
Otis invented a solution:
the safety elevator. At the
1854 World's Fair in New
York, he climbed into
an elevator in front of a
crowd of people. Then
he cut right through the
cable. The elevator fell
only a few feet before his
safety device stopped it.
People were convinced,
and architects began
putting elevators into
their buildings.

Elevators wouldn't work for tall skyscrapers, though. They were too slow. No one wanted to wait ten or fifteen minutes to get up to the twenty-fifth floor. So in 1878, Otis came up with an elevator that could travel eight stories in less than a minute. His inventions made skyscrapers practical. Otis is still the world's largest elevator maker. If you look at the floor when you get into an elevator, chances are it will say *Otis*.

Elisha Otis

The Importance of Elevators

The number of elevators that can fit in a building helps decide how tall it can be. The more floors there are, the more elevators will be needed to carry people to them. But elevators take up a lot of floor space. If there are too many of them, there won't be any room left for offices or apartments. Architects have to work out the perfect height for a building. They try to find the point when there are exactly enough elevators for the floor space that is left. The Empire State Building today has seventy-three elevators.

Space is very valuable in New York. Owners want to use as much of their lot as possible. Even before skyscrapers, this meant that many streets were solid blocks of stone from end to end. There was no space between one building and the next.

This hadn't really mattered when the buildings were short. But now skyscrapers were springing up everywhere. By 1929, there were 188 buildings in New York that were over twenty stories high. This led to a new problem. Imagine an unbroken line of buildings, all skyscrapers twenty stories tall. The sun would never reach the streets. They would become deep gullies where howling winds would knock down anyone who tried to walk in them.

To prevent this, in 1916, New York City created the nation's first zoning laws. The laws said that after a building reached a certain height, it had to have a *setback*, a step in, so the building got smaller. As it got taller, it had to keep adding setbacks. So as a building rose, it had to get thinner and narrower. Setbacks made sure that some sun would reach the streets and there would be sky between tall towers. At any point, the builder could stop using setbacks and build a tower. Then there was no limit on how high the tower could be. However, it could be no bigger around than one-quarter of the building's lot.

Setback

Most architects wanted buildings they could be proud of. So they experimented with ways to arrange setbacks that were interesting to look at. They topped their buildings with towers like church steeples. The 1916 zoning law created the famous New York skyline we know today—a city of pyramids, towers, and soaring spires.

CHAPTER 4
The Happy Warrior

It was clear that anything built on the Waldorf-Astoria site would have to be tall. The land was too valuable for anything else. But no one had yet designed a tall building in such a huge lot.

The buyers hired architects who designed an ordinary fifty-story skyscraper. They planned to call it the Waldorf-Astoria Office Building. Then they lost interest. With so many other skyscrapers going up, they were afraid there would be too much new office space. Maybe they wouldn't be able to rent theirs. So they sold the land.

The group that bought it was headed by John Jakob Raskob. He was one of the richest men in America. He had worked for General Motors until he got into political trouble and had to resign. Raskob was so rich that he could have done nothing for the rest of his life. But he liked to keep busy. And he wanted to make sure that what went up on the site of the old Waldorf-Astoria Hotel was worthy of the spot.

Raskob brought in his friend Al Smith to be president of the building company. Al Smith was the former governor of New York State. He was also one of the most popular men in the city. His nickname was "the Happy Warrior." When Smith was enthusiastic about anything, he wanted to share it with his fellow New Yorkers. His excitement was catching because it was so real.

John Jakob Raskob   Al Smith

Smith was a real New York City boy. Ordinary New Yorkers thought of him as one of their own. He was born to an Irish Catholic family in a poor neighborhood. As a child, he sold newspapers on the streets. At fifteen, he started working long hours at the Fulton Fish Market. He never went to college. He always said that he got his education at the fish market.

He broke into politics with the help of local Irish politicians. Al Smith liked people, and he liked helping them. So he quickly became a very successful politician. He was elected governor of New York State four times, and served from 1919 to 1920 and from 1923 to 1928.

Al Smith and the Triangle Shirtwaist Factory

The working-class people of New York started to think of Al Smith as *their* politician after the tragic Triangle Shirtwaist Factory disaster of 1911. The factory caught fire, and the workers found themselves trapped inside. The owners had locked the building's fire escape exits to make sure no one tried to sneak out. People jumped from the windows, hoping to escape. One hundred forty-six clothing workers, mostly young women, were killed. After the fire, Al Smith helped lead the fight to pass stronger laws that would protect workers.

Al Smith wanted to run for president. However, too many people wouldn't even consider voting for anyone Catholic. In 1928, after he was passed over for the second time, he gave up politics. He found himself at loose ends.

According to one story, Raskob overhcard Al Smith in the men's room at a party. He was fretting about what to do next. Raskob told him not to worry. He said he was going to build the biggest skyscraper in the world, and make Smith president of the company.

The newspapers had already been following the fate of the Waldorf-Astoria site. But once Al Smith joined, it became big news. On August 30, 1929, the *New York Times* headline read: SMITH TO HELP BUILD HIGHEST SKYSCRAPER. This article was one of the first to call the building the Empire State Building. The name was probably Smith's idea. "The Empire State" was a common nickname for New York. With Smith in charge, it was sure to be the tallest, most beautiful, and most famous building ever. It was only natural for him to name it after his beloved New York.

SMITH TO HELP BUILD HIGHEST SKYSCRAPER

Ex-Governor Heads Group That Will Put 80-Story Office Building on Waldorf Site.

COST PUT AT $60,000,000

He Will Be President and Have Executive Control of Concern Yet to Be Incorporated.

Why the "Empire" State?

No one knows who nicknamed New York the Empire State. An *empire* is a group of countries or states under one ruler, so no single state can truly be an empire. The name may have come from George Washington. In a letter written in 1785, he described New York City as "the seat of the Empire." He meant that, at the time, the city was the capital of the United States. To Al Smith, it must have seemed appropriate to use the state's nickname for the world's tallest building—especially because the state motto, *Excelsior*, means "always upward."

CHAPTER 5
A Building Shaped Like a Pencil

The new owners asked for a new building design from the same architects who made the first design. The company was called Shreve, Lamb and Harmon. William Lamb was the main designer.

William Lamb

Raskob and Smith told Lamb they wanted something more unusual and elegant. It should soar upward. Raskob took his pencil, point up, and stood it on end. He wanted the building to look like that. "How high can you make it so that it won't fall down?" he asked.

Lamb came up with a beautiful new design. He decided to make only the first five floors the size of the full lot. Then there was a very large setback. To people walking on the street, the building would seem friendly and human-size.

After the sixth floor setback, the tower started. To beat the Chrysler Building, the tower would go up to the eighty-sixth floor. Because the site was so big and the first setback so dramatic, the huge tower would look slender and elegant.

The slender tower was much smaller than the wide building that could have fit there. So, there was less office space to rent. But space in the tower was very valuable. In the 1930s, natural daylight was important for office buildings. If the upper floors had been made as big as possible, much of the space would have been very far away from windows. It would have been difficult to rent at a good price. Now most of the building was in the tower. All offices would be near a window. And they would all be set back far enough from the street to be quiet. They could be rented for a lot more money.

The company hoped to rent out some whole floors to single businesses. But it was also willing to rent single-room offices. It planned to leave the space unfinished on the inside, so that each renter could make his office any size or shape he wanted.

Lamb had created the pencil-shaped building Smith and Raskob wanted. But something still wasn't quite right. The top of the tower was flat and looked a little stubby. Al Smith was famous for wearing a round brown derby hat. He and Raskob thought the building needed a hat, too. The architect tried designing a dome, but a little round top on such a huge tower looked silly.

Then one of the men came up with an insane idea. They would build a special feature that would add two hundred feet to the height of the building. The addition would show what modern thinkers the building's owners were. The world would see that they were planning a building for the future.

Smith announced the crazy new idea to the newspapers in December 1929. He said that the top of the building would be a mooring mast for flying ships! *Dirigibles*—enormous floating balloons that could be steered—would dock there.

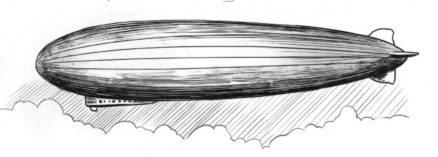

People thought that one day passengers would be flying all over the world in dirigibles. But they were so enormous that it was hard to find anyplace to dock them. Al Smith imagined them floating right up to his building. The passengers would walk down a gangplank on the 102nd floor and then take the elevator to the ground floor. And there they would be, in the heart of Manhattan.

It was an absolutely impossible idea. Who would risk walking down an open gangplank so high up in the air? That far up, the wind would be very unpredictable. (Workers in the upper offices of the Empire State Building can sometimes watch snow falling *upward*.) A huge, floating balloon tied to the mooring mast would bounce around like a bucking bronco.

Al Smith may have really hoped that his building would become a station for flying ships. Or the idea might have been just a publicity stunt. In any case, it never happened.

A tall, slender mooring mast was added to the top of the building. This made its final height 102 floors and 1,250 feet—much taller than the

Chrysler Building. But no dirigibles ever really docked there. However, the spire did not go to waste. As the highest place in the city, it turned out to be the perfect spot for radio and television broadcasts. It is still used for that purpose.

Trying to Dock at the Mooring Mast

Dirigibles only came near the Empire State Building's mast three times. Once, as a favor to Al Smith, a navy dirigible hovered near the mast long enough to be filmed, and then flew away. Once, one dropped a stack of newspapers onto the roof of the building. And one time, a small dirigible actually managed to dock. After trying for half an hour, it got close enough for the crew to throw a rope to the men waiting on top of the building. They fastened the rope to the mast, and were able to keep it there for three whole minutes before they had to cut it loose. But nobody could get off or on.

CHAPTER 6
Blasting Away the Astor Hotel

With the design settled, the company needed to hire a building firm. They chose Starrett Brothers and Eken. This firm was known for building safely and honestly. Starrett Brothers also promised to have the Empire State Building finished and ready for tenants by May 1, 1931. That meant getting rid of a huge hotel and replacing it with the world's tallest skyscraper in only a year and a half.

Why were Raskob and Smith in such a hurry?

Most leases for offices in New York began on either May 1 or November 1. So it made sense for the Empire State Building to open for business on one of those two days. That way, it could fill up right away. If they missed May 1, they would have to wait another six months. Every day offices sat empty meant money lost. Also, Smith knew that the newspapers would love the race to meet the date. It would be good publicity.

The first step was destroying the old hotel. On October 1, 1929, Al Smith himself began the process. In front of a crowd of cameras, he pulled a special rope. It brought down ten feet of copper decoration. The rest of the destruction was not so easy. The Waldorf-Astoria was enormous and had been built to last. Daredevils called *barmen* stood on top of a section of wall. They loosened the bricks with an iron bar. Then they jumped off

before the wall collapsed under them. The steel framework had to be cut apart and removed with flaming torches.

This left a huge amount of trash. Some of it was bought by souvenir collectors who wanted a memory of the famous old hotel. Some of it could be recycled. The builders held on to anything they could use to help build the skyscraper. For instance, the hotel elevators were left in place and used to haul building materials up to higher floors.

To get rid of wooden trash, Smith had a clever idea. He gave it away for free to poor people who used it to heat their homes. The wood didn't have to be hauled away, and it was good publicity. Still, a lot of trash was left. The builders found that the cheapest thing to do was to load it on barges, sail away from the harbor, and then dump it. Today, most of the grand old hotel lies at the bottom of the Atlantic Ocean.

The next step was digging the foundation. Two shifts of three hundred workers each worked twenty-four hours a day, blasting away the earth and rock with dynamite. They needed to make a huge, deep hole. The steel bars holding up the building would be set in concrete blocks going all the way down to the earth's bedrock. About forty feet down, the builders hit a layer of the rock called *Manhattan schist*. It is one of the strongest kinds of bedrock. This was a lucky thing. The world's tallest building would weigh around 365,000 tons, so it needed a good, strong foundation to hold it up.

CHAPTER 7
A Framework of Steel

After the foundation hole was blasted, actual construction began. It was a very complicated process. Because the building had to be finished so quickly, everything and everyone had to be in the right place the second they were needed. If one step broke down, everything after it would be delayed. It took careful planning.

The construction was divided into a series of different steps that had to be done in order. Building the steel framework was the first step. Builders started at the bottom and worked their way up, floor by floor. As soon as possible, another group of workers

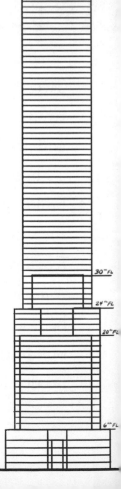

would begin the second step at the bottom, following the first group up. Then the third step would start at the bottom, and so on. One of the architects explained, "We always thought of it as a parade in which each marcher kept pace and the parade marched out of the top of the building, still in perfect step."

When the builders ordered the steel framework, Raskob took a big risk. New York's laws about building with steel were out-of-date. When they were made, lawmakers hadn't known how strong and flexible this material was. So the laws called for a lot more steel than was really needed to make buildings safe. There had been talk about changing the laws, but it hadn't happened yet.

Between them, Raskob and Smith had a lot of rich and powerful friends. They gambled that they could get the laws changed before actual construction began on the Empire State Building. So they ordered a lighter—and cheaper—steel framework that didn't obey the laws. If they lost this bet, they would be stuck with a lot of beams they couldn't use. But they won. The laws were changed in time.

To make the framework, the builders first set up 210 vertical steel columns. Twelve of them ran the entire height of the main building, from the foundation to the eighty-sixth floor. Then horizontal steel beams were added to hold them in place and help carry weight. Each beam was hoisted up and swung into position by men perched on the beams that were already there. They strolled casually along these narrow metal bars as if they didn't care how high up they were.

The framework was fastened together with red-hot steel rivets. When the rivets cooled, the joint would be as solid as if it were one piece. It was very important for rivets to be well made. A bad rivet could weaken the whole structure. (Many scientists now believe that badly made rivets caused the *Titanic* to break apart and sink.)

Riveters worked in teams of four. The team members trained together and always worked with one another. Standing on a floor that was partly finished, the *passer* heated the rivets in a forge.

Then he used tongs to throw them up as high as seventy-five feet to the floors above. There, the *catcher* caught them in an old paint can. The *bucker-up* then steadied the rivet in place, while the *gunman* hit it with a special hammer. The hammer was powered by compressed air, and it forced the rivet into the hole, where it fused with the steel beam. All of this had to be done very quickly, before the rivet cooled.

The process of erecting the framework was so well organized that the builders were able to put up an entire story or more in one day. The very last rivet was shot by Al Smith himself. It was not made of steel but of solid gold.

CHAPTER 8
One Year and Forty-Five Days Later

New Yorkers loved watching the huge building go up. It was the best free entertainment in town. For these watchers, called *sidewalk superintendents*, the blasting, ironwork, and riveting were the most exciting steps. After that, the work moved inside the building's frame, and there wasn't as much to see. There was still a lot to be done, though.

The stone curtain wall had to be hung from the steel. Electricity and plumbing had to be put in, and the inside floors, walls, and ceilings finished.

To stay on schedule, everything had to move like clockwork. The building was put together using prebuilt pieces—like window frames or wall sections—that were all exactly like one another.

These pieces could be put together somewhere else, and then delivered to the building site ready to be put into place. Pieces were numbered to tell the workers where they should go. Complicated schedules made sure each one was delivered to the building site exactly when the builders were ready to install it. There was no storage space at the construction site, so there would be nowhere to put a piece that came too early.

Lifting heavy pieces, like walls, to where they belonged was hard work. Most builders used cranes standing outside the building to lift materials into place. But at the Empire State Building site, after the steel structure was finished, nothing above the first five floors was lifted up by cranes. Instead, all the material rode up in elevators inside the building. There was a little railroad on each floor. Train tracks ran from the elevators to every corner of the building. Once something reached the right

floor, it traveled to where it belonged on a hand-operated railroad car.

As the building got taller, getting the men all the way up to where they needed to work started to take a long time. At noon, many men didn't want to waste half their lunchtime traveling all the way down to the ground floor to buy lunch. So the company set up cafeterias serving cheap, hot food on five floors inside the unfinished building.

It was a huge operation. More than three thousand men might be at work at the same time. They were busy moving tons of material, operating heavy machines, and walking around on open floors high above the street.

Working in the building trade was more dangerous than any other industry except mining. Rumors flew about how many people were killed during the construction of the Empire State Building. It was said that one person had to die for each floor that was built. Actually, the builders took safety very seriously. Everything was planned to make sure there was no unnecessary risk. And there was a first-aid hospital right in the unfinished building, just in case. From beginning to end, only five men were killed. This was still too many—the Chrysler Building had gone up without a single worker being killed. But it was an impressive record.

All Starrett Brothers' careful planning and problem solving paid off. The timetable had seemed impossibly fast. It could work only if everything went perfectly. And everything did. The building was not finished on time. It was finished *early*. From the start of the demolition to the finishing touches on the world's tallest building, it took only one year and forty-five days.

CHAPTER 9
Depressing Times

The Empire State Building's record for safety and speed would have been impressive at any time. It was even more amazing considering what was happening in the rest of the country. When the building was first planned, the United States was going through a period of wealth. Investors were becoming very rich. People thought anyone who worked hard could succeed.

Then everything changed. In October 1929, the stock market crashed. It plunged the United States and the western world into ten years of poverty called the Great Depression. Huge fortunes disappeared overnight. Banks failed. Many ordinary people lost everything they owned. Eventually, 25 percent of Americans were out of work.

The crash took place only a month after the demolition of the Waldorf-Astoria started. Raskob was very lucky. He did not lose his whole fortune. But he was risking a lot of his money to erect the world's tallest building. It might have made more sense to drop the idea—or at least build something smaller and less expensive. Instead, Raskob decided to go ahead.

Raskob gathered together a group of investors. Supporting projects like the Empire State Building, he explained, showed their belief in the United States. He was sure the country could make it through the crisis. But people who still had money had to help. They couldn't be afraid to spend their money on public projects.

Building the Empire State Building was clearly a good thing for the country during the Great Depression. It employed thousands of local workers. And its need for steel, stone, and other construction materials helped keep factories going all over the country. After it opened, the Empire State Building would still create jobs. It would need a staff of at least three hundred people just to run it.

The Great Depression turned out to be a good thing for the Empire State Building, in some ways. Prices for construction materials dropped so much that the building came in millions of dollars under budget. With so many people out of work, the builders could hire the very best people. Workers were grateful for a good job and eager to do it well.

The Depression also helped the Empire State Building keep its title as the world's tallest building for so many years. Other grand building projects had been planned. But these projects were dropped because there was no money for them. By the time the Depression ended, World War II was beginning. All of the country's resources were needed for the war. So for a long time, no one dreamed of challenging the Empire State Building's record.

CHAPTER 10
Filling the Empty State Building

On May 1, 1931, Al Smith's two young grandchildren cut the red ribbon at the entrance of the Empire State Building. At the same time, in Washington, DC, President Herbert Hoover pressed a button. In New York City, the lights in the lobby turned on. The crowds rushed in and the building officially opened.

But the ceremony hid a sad fact. Everywhere in New York, businesses were closing. No one needed new office space. There weren't enough people with jobs to fill the offices in older buildings. When the Empire State Building opened, fewer than a quarter of the offices inside had anyone in them. Raskob's office on the eightieth floor must have been very lonely. Below it there were thirty-eight empty floors before you reached the women's underwear company on the forty-

first floor. People began to call the building the "Empty State Building."

Still, everyone wanted to see the view from the top. For a dollar—twenty-five cents for children—you could ride up to the eighty-sixth floor. (Children under five got in for free.) There, you could eat at "the world's highest tearoom and soda fountain." Then you could take another elevator to the 102nd floor, where on a clear day, you could see eighty miles in all directions.

The view included five states—New York, Connecticut, Massachusetts, Pennsylvania, and New Jersey—and ships far out at sea.

The first Sunday after the opening, 5,108 people paid to go to the top. For most of the Great Depression, the viewing platforms were one of the building's main sources of income. Any day the weather was good, about 3,000 people visited.

Al Smith was the building's "host." He loved
greeting celebrities—or anyone else he happened
to meet. Famous people who visited the building
in its early years includes Helen Keller; the great
female pilot Amelia Earhart; Robert Wadlow,
the world's tallest man; the king of Siam; and
Lassie, the movie-star dog. Smith did everything

he could to keep the building in the news. In 1937, the newspapers reported on the first time anyone officially walked up the stairs all the way to the top. A farmer from Vermont climbed the 1,860 steps in thirty-six minutes. He remarked that "mountains are harder to climb." But he was not really the first. Two small boys had already sneaked past a security guard and made the climb.

(Since 1978, the building has hosted an annual race up the 1,576 steps to the eighty-sixth floor. The winner usually takes about ten minutes.)

To keep visitors coming, Smith and his agents came up with many publicity stunts. They arranged for a séance to be held on the eighty-sixth floor. A group of people would gather and try to talk to the spirits of dead people. The idea was that, up so high, ghosts who wanted to communicate wouldn't have to fight with radio signals. In 1933, they planned for a groundhog to appear on top of the building on Groundhog Day. But it escaped and ran away. Many radio specials were broadcast from the eighty-sixth floor, as well as a regular program interviewing the building's visitors. It was called *The Microphone in the Sky*.

King Kong

The Empire State Building got a big boost when *King Kong* came out in 1933. In this movie, a giant ape escapes in New York City. He falls in love with a beautiful blonde and carries her up to the spire of the Empire State Building. The scene of a giant ape carrying the screaming girl in one hand became very famous. Actually, the movie did not show the real Empire State Building. It used a miniature model with a miniature ape. On the fiftieth anniversary of the movie, a giant, eighty-four-foot gorilla-shaped balloon was attached to the spire of the building for a week.

After the United States entered World War II in 1941, people were afraid that New York City might be a bombing target. Guards in the observatory of the Empire State Building watched for enemy airplanes. All the building's lights were blacked out above the fifteenth floor at night. The government was afraid the light would make ships at sea an easier target. However, the building's worst involvement in the war was a strange and tragic accident.

On July 28, 1945, an experienced army pilot was flying some soldiers to New Jersey in a B-25 bomber. The weather was terrible, with rain and thick, low clouds. The pilot got lost. To see where he was, he flew down below the cloud level. To his horror he discovered that he was in midtown Manhattan, surrounded by skyscrapers. He did his best to steer around them, but it was impossible. The plane smashed into the seventy-ninth floor of the Empire State Building and burst into flames. Eleven people were killed in the building, plus the three on the plane.

A gaping hole was torn from the seventy-eighth to the eightieth floors. The airplane's engine shot right through all the offices and out the other side. Even so, most of the building was undamaged. It was open for business again in only two days. Though it was terrible, the accident showed how well made the building was.

CHAPTER 11
A Lost World Record

The years after World War II were good ones for the Empire State Building. It quickly filled with tenants. And it kept finding new ways to hold the public's interest.

Starting in the 1960s, the Empire State Building invited two Boy Scout troops each year to camp out overnight. They pitched their tents on the marble floors of the eighty-sixth floor observatory deck. In the 1970s, Girl Scouts began to camp there, as well.

Another popular innovation was nighttime lighting on the outside of the building. The first permanent lights were four revolving white beacons at the base of the spire. Added in 1956, these were called the Freedom Lights. In 1964, they were replaced by floodlights that lit up the

entire top of the building. In 1976, the lights were colored red, white, and blue for the United States' two hundredth birthday. People liked the colors so much that the building decided to keep them. Today, different colors are used to honor

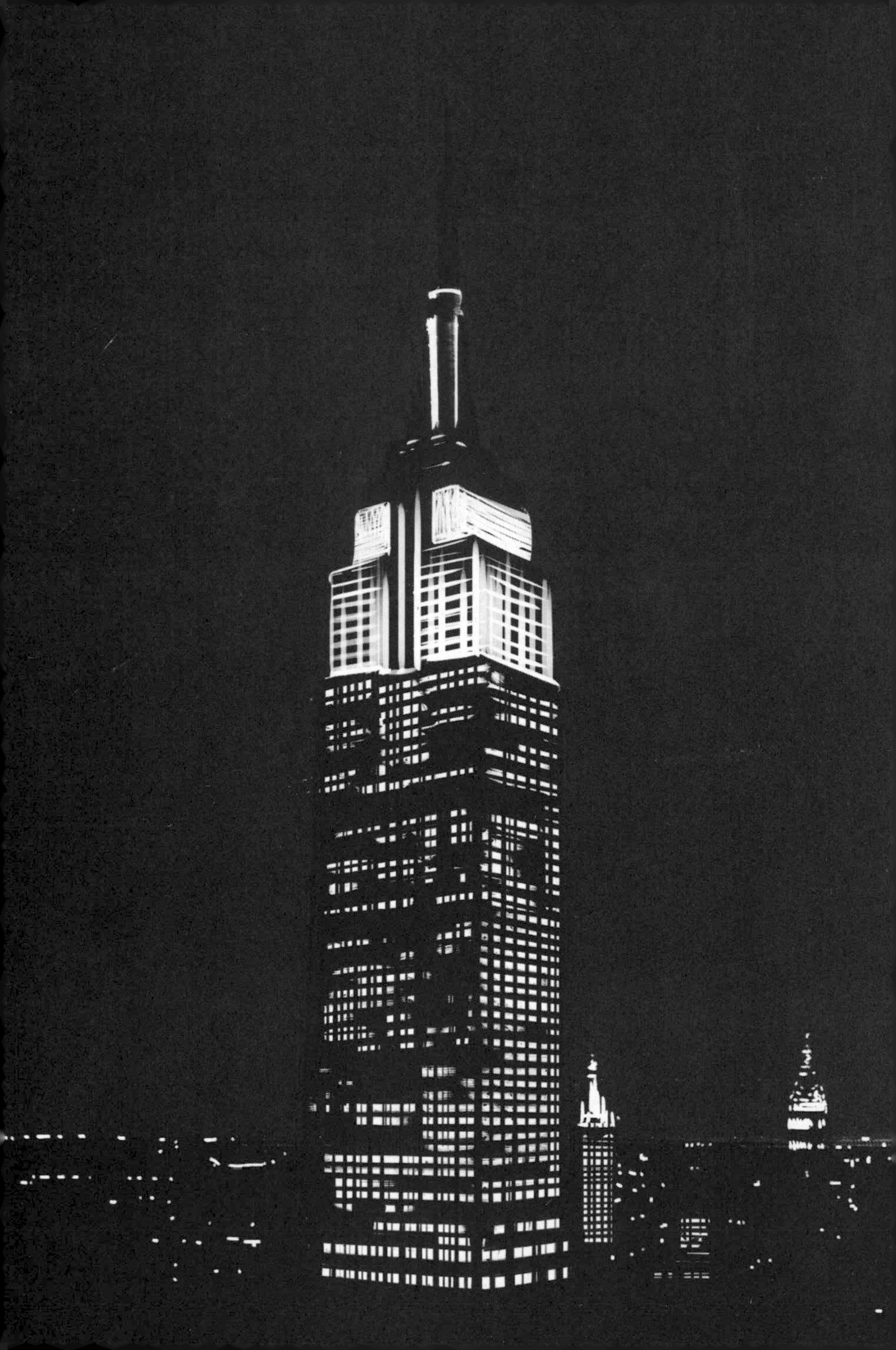

various days. Before Christmas, the lights are red and green. Before a big baseball game, they might be the colors of a New York team. For years, the colors had to be changed by hand, by putting gel covers over the white lights. In 2012, the building switched to LED lights. These can be programmed. Now the building can put on light shows where the colors ripple and change. During the season when birds are migrating, the lights are turned off at midnight so that they won't confuse any passing birds.

In 1950, a new antenna was added to the top of the spire for radio and television broadcasting. The new antenna increased the building's height by 217 feet. However, even this new addition could not stop the Empire State Building from losing its world record.

In the 1960s, plans began for the World Trade Center in lower Manhattan. Two of the center's towers were planned to be taller than the Empire

State Building. The owners of the Empire State Building wanted to keep the title of the world's tallest building. So they came up with a plan to take off the top and add on eleven more stories. Instead of trying to match the style of the original building, the new top would be modern. Fortunately, this plan was dropped. The famous silhouette of the Empire State Building remained untouched.

In 1971, before it was even finished, One World Trade Center became the world's tallest building. In 1972, Two World Trade Center became the second tallest. Although New Yorkers were proud of them, the Twin Towers did not inspire the same kind of affection that the Empire State Building had. They were plain, giant rectangles, rising straight up to a flat top. People said they looked like the boxes that the Empire State Building and the Chrysler Building had been delivered in.

Only two years after the Twin Towers took

away the record, they lost it as well. In 1973, the Sears Tower in Chicago became the world's tallest building. It held the record for twenty-five years. Then the title moved out of the United States altogether. In 1998, the Petronas Towers in Kuala Lumpur, Malaysia, became the world's tallest, followed by the Taipei World Financial Center in Taiwan in 2004, and then Burj Khalifa in Dubai in 2010.

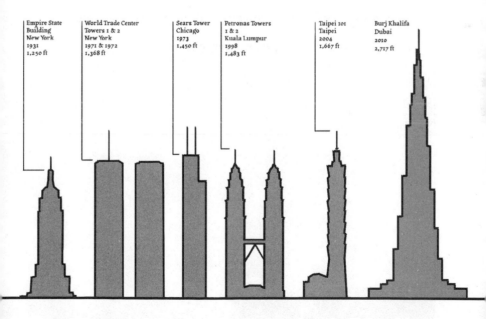

Empire State
Building
New York
1931
1,250 ft

World Trade Center
Towers 1 & 2
New York
1971 & 1972
1,368 ft

Sears Tower
Chicago
1973
1,450 ft

Petronas Towers
1 & 2
Kuala Lumpur
1998
1,483 ft

Taipei 101
Taipei
2004
1,667 ft

Burj Khalifa
Dubai
2010
2,717 ft

The Green Empire State Building

In 2009, the Empire State Building was renovated. During the process, it became a "green" building—one that protects the environment as much as possible. The building's use of energy was cut by almost 40 percent. And it began buying all of its electricity from a company that uses windmills to generate power. In 2011, the building won Leadership in Energy and Environmental Design (LEED) Gold certification in honor of its achievement.

CHAPTER 12
Close to Heaven

In 2001, the two towers of the World Trade Center were destroyed by a terrorist attack. Suddenly the Empire State Building was again the tallest building in New York. People were afraid it might also be a target for terrorists. Security was increased. Today, all visitors must show ID and pass through a metal detector. The building also uses special video cameras and bomb-sniffing dogs.

The Empire State Building remained the tallest building in New York until 2012. Then the new One World Trade Center passed it, continuing to rise until it overtook the Sears Tower as well to become the tallest building in the United States. The Empire State Building will never be the world's tallest building—or even New York's tallest—again.

But somehow, it still holds a place in people's hearts that no other building does. It continues to receive almost four million visitors a year—more than any of the buildings that have passed it in height. In 2007, a national poll named it America's favorite building. For people everywhere, it will always be, as it is called in the classic movie *An Affair to Remember*, "the nearest thing to heaven we have in New York."

Timeline of the Empire State Building

1827	William Astor buys the land where the Empire State Building will one day stand
1856	Building of the Astor mansions on the site begins
1893	One Astor mansion is replaced by the Waldorf Hotel
1897	The other Astor mansion is replaced by the Astoria Hotel, which is connected to the Waldorf Hotel
1913	The Woolworth Building in Manhattan becomes the world's tallest skyscraper
1928	The site of the Waldorf-Astoria Hotel is sold to developers for about $16 million
1929	Demolition of Waldorf-Astoria begins
1930	Construction of the Empire State Building begins
1931	The Empire State Building is completed after one year and forty-five days of construction
1933	The movie *King Kong* shows a giant gorilla climbing the building
1937	A Vermont farmer walks up 1,860 stairs to the top of the building
1945	An airplane smashes into the seventy-ninth floor of the building due to fog
1950	A radio antenna is added, increasing the building's height by 217 feet
1956	The first permanent lights, called "The Freedom Lights," are installed outside the building
1962	The outside of the building is cleaned for the first time
1976	The outside of the building is lit in color for the first time
	The observatory receives its fifty millionth visitor
1978	The building begins hosting an annual race up the stairs
1986	The Empire State Building is named a National Historic Landmark
2001	The Empire State Building is again the tallest building in New York
2011	The building wins a Leadership in Energy and Environmental Design (LEED®) Gold

Timeline of the World

The world's first modern railroad opens in England — **1825**
First building in the United States with a complete — **1850**
cast-iron frame is built in New York
Elisha Otis invents the safety elevator — **1852**
Henry Bessemer patents a new method of making steel — **1855**
The American Civil War begins — **1861**
The world's first skyscraper is built in Chicago — **1885**
The *Titanic* sinks. Among those killed is John Jacob Astor IV. — **1912**
Hearings are held in the Waldorf-Astoria
World War I begins — **1914**
Alfred E. Smith is elected governor — **1918**
of New York for the first time
The stock market crashes, beginning the Great Depression — **1929**
The new Waldorf-Astoria opens on Park Avenue — **1931**
Franklin Delano Roosevelt is elected president and begins — **1932**
his "New Deal" aimed at ending the Depression
Adolf Hitler's Nazi party comes to power in Germany — **1933**
The United States enters World War II — **1941**
The Soviet Union launches the satellite *Sputnik I* into space — **1957**
Alaska and Hawaii become states — **1959**
One World Trade Center passes the Empire State Building — **1970**
to become the world's tallest building
United States agrees to withdraw from Vietnam — **1973**
The Sears Tower in Chicago becomes —
the world's tallest building
The Cold War ends with the breakup of the Soviet Union — **1991**
Terrorists destroy the World Trade Center — **2001**
The newly built One World Trade Center passes the Empire — **2012**
State Building to become the tallest building in New York

Bibliography

*Books for young readers

Douglas, George H. *Skyscrapers: A Social History of the Very
Tall Building in America.* Jefferson, NC: McFarland &
Company, 1996.

*Macaulay, David. *Unbuilding.* Boston: Houghton Mifflin, 1980.

*Mann, Elizabeth. *Empire State Building.* Wonders of the World.
New York: Mikaya Press, 2003.

"Empire State Building/Lewis W. Hines." New York Public Library
Digital Gallery http://digitalcollections.nypl.org

Tauranac, John. *The Empire State Building: The Making of a
Landmark.* New York: Scribner, 1995.

Willis, Carol, editor. *Building the Empire State Building.* New
York: W. W. Norton, in association with the Skyscraper
Museum, 1998.